OUR GOVERNMENT

The Supreme Court
and the Judicial Branch

Bryon Giddens-White

Heinemann
LIBRARY

Chicago, Illinois

Customer Service 888-454-2279

Visit our website at www.heinemannlibrary.com

Designed by David Poole and Calcium
Illustrations by Geoff Ward
Originated by P.T. Repro Multi Warna
Printed in China by WKT Company Limited

07 06 05
10 9 8 7 6 5 4 3 2 1

Library of Congress Cataloging-in-Publication Data
Library of Congress Cataloging-in-Publication Data

Giddens-White, Bryon.
  The Supreme Court and the judicial branch / Bryon Giddens-White.
      p. cm. -- (Our government)
  Includes bibliographical references and index.
  ISBN 1-4034-6603-3 (hc) -- ISBN 1-4034-6608-4 (pb)
  1. United States. Supreme Court--Juvenile literature. 2. Judicial power--United States--Juvenile Literature. I. Title.
  KF8742.Z9G53 2006
  347.73'26--dc22
                        2005008666

Acknowledgments
AP Wide World Photo pp. 25, 28, 29 (J. Scott Applewhite); Corbis pp. 5 (Bettmann), 6 (Bettmann), 9 (Stapleton Collection), 16 (Franklin McMahon), 17 (Sygma/Soqui Ted), 19 (Reuters/Pool/Paul Sakuma), 20 (Bettmann), 22 (Franklin McMahon), 24 (Bettmann), 26 (Bettmann), 27 (Sygma/Bowe Christy); Getty Images pp. 1 (Taxi/Peter Gridley), p. 21 (Time Life Pictures/Margaret Bourke White); Heinemann Library p. 18 (Greg Williams); National Archives and Records Administration p. 7; The Granger Collection, New York pp. 10, 13.

Cover photograph of the Supreme Court Building reproduced with permission of Getty Images (Taxi/Peter Gridley.)

Special thanks to David G. Barnum and Gary Barr for their help in the production of this book.

Contents

Any words appearing in the text in bold, **like this**, are explained in the Glossary.

The Supreme Court Upholds the Right to Free Speech

What would you do if one day, your school told you that you weren't allowed to express your beliefs? In 1965, three students faced that question. They stood up for their right to free speech, and they took their school to court. Their case was eventually heard by the U.S. **Supreme Court**, the highest court of the United States government.

During the 1960s, the United States sent soldiers to fight a war in Vietnam, a country in Southeast Asia. By the late 1960s, citizens who believed that the war was a mistake began to protest in large numbers. Young people, including several public school students in Des Moines, Iowa, also joined the protest movement. Mary Beth and John Tinker and Christopher Eckhardt were among those students. They planned to wear black armbands to school to express their sadness over the soldiers and civilians hurt or killed in Vietnam.

School officials heard about the plan, and worried that the students' protest would cause trouble in the school. They created a new rule that said that students who wore armbands to school would be asked to remove them. They threatened to suspend students who did not obey.

Even though the three students knew about the rule, they went ahead with their plan. When they got to school, school officials asked them to

▲ Mary Beth and John Tinker display the armbands they wore to protest the Vietnam War.

remove their armbands. The Tinkers and Christopher Eckhardt refused, and the officials suspended them. The students' families believed their children had a right to free expression, so they took the case to court.

The case went all the way to the Supreme Court, and in 1969 it sided with the students. The Court ruled that the students' actions were unlikely to cause trouble. In their decision, the Supreme Court **justices** said that wearing armbands was a form of free speech, a right that is protected by the U.S. **Constitution**.

Today, the Supreme Court continues to make decisions about how laws are applied in our daily lives. In this book, you will learn more about the Supreme Court and the **judicial branch** of the U.S. government.

Introduction to the Judicial Branch

Fact File

Location of Supreme Court: Washington, D.C.

Number of Justices: Nine (one **chief justice** and eight associate justices)

Appointment: The president nominates Supreme Court justices, but the Senate must approve the president's choices.

Term of Office: Life

Salary: Chief Justice: $203,000; Associate Justice: $194,300

Length of Court Term: About 38 weeks—from the first Monday in October until late June or early July

During the spring of 1787, a group of men gathered to make a plan for the government of the United States. The written document that they created is called a constitution. Constitutions describe the powers and duties of a country's government. They also contain important laws, such as those that protect the rights of the country's citizens.

The U.S. Constitution divides the government into three branches, or parts. The three branches are the **legislative branch**, the **executive branch**, and the judicial branch. The legislative branch makes the laws. The executive branch carries out and enforces the laws. The judicial branch interprets the laws and makes sure that they agree with the Constitution.

The Constitution divides the judicial branch into the Supreme Court and several lower courts, which are established by the legislative branch. It is the job of the judicial branch to make certain that every U.S. citizen is equally protected under the laws defined by the Constitution.

◀ A large number of individuals worked together to write the Constitution. However, they paid a clerk from Pennsylvania named Jacob Shallus $30 to pen the final draft.

◀ Men from all over the United States traveled to Philadelphia in 1787. They made a plan for the U.S. government that we still use today—the Constitution.

The Constitution and the Judicial Branch

Knowing that the nation would change over time and that problems would arise that they could never imagine, the authors of the Constitution wrote it to be a flexible document open to discussion. They laid out basic ideas, such as the right of every citizen to speak freely, but did not specifically describe them. In this way, the ideas could be debated and interpreted to meet the needs of the United States over time. This is one reason why the U.S. Constitution is the oldest written constitution still in use anywhere in the world.

The **federal** courts are responsible for interpreting the constitution and applying it to court cases. This is a major responsibility, and the authors of the Constitution wanted to make certain that every federal judge could be trusted to make the fairest, most honest decisions possible. They developed a plan to ensure that the federal court system treated everyone equally.

Article Five:

While the judicial branch interprets the constitution, the legislative branch has the power to change it. Article Five of the U.S. Constitution describes the process of changing, or amending, the Constitution. It provides two methods of proposing amendments. In the first method, Congress can propose an amendment by a two-thirds majority vote in each house. The Constitution can also be amended through action by the states. If two-thirds of the state legislatures agree, they can request a convention to discuss possible amendments. The amendments must then be ratified, or approved, by three-fourths of the states in order to take effect.

First, the framers decided that justices would be appointed for life. This way, justices can make decisions without worrying about losing their jobs if their decisions are unpopular. Second, they decided that the amount of money justices earn should remain the same throughout their **term** so that no one could persuade a justice to rule a certain way by offering to raise his or her pay. These plans helped ensure that federal justices would make decisions based upon their understanding of the Constitution, not public opinion or pressure from politicians.

◀ The head justice of the Supreme Court is called the chief justice. The longest-serving chief justice was John Marshall, who held the position for 34 years.

Judicial Checks and Balances

The authors of the Constitution did not want the national government to have too much power. They decided to give certain powers to the national government and other powers to the state governments. This is called a **federal system** of government. They further divided the national government into three branches, creating a **separation of powers**. Finally, they created a system in which each branch could check, or limit, the powers of the other branches. In this way, a balance of power would exist among the three branches. This is called a system of **checks and balances**.

Judicial and Legislative Checks

One of the checks held by the judicial branch is **judicial review**, which is the Supreme Court's power to declare a law **unconstitutional** if it violates the Constitution. This gives the judicial branch a powerful check on the laws created by the legislative branch.

The legislative branch has checks on the judicial branch as well. Although federal judges are appointed for life, they cannot take office until

Judicial Review

Judicial review was established in 1803 by the case *Marbury vs. Madison*. Just before leaving office, President John Adams appointed to office a large number of people, including William Marbury (pictured above), who shared Adams' political views. The next president did not share Adams' views and asked his secretary of state, James Madison, to prevent some of Adams' appointments, including Marbury's. Marbury sued Madison, but the court ruled against Marbury. The justices said that the law used by Marbury to demand his position—a provision of the Judiciary Act of 1789—was unconstitutional.

Judicial Checks and Balances

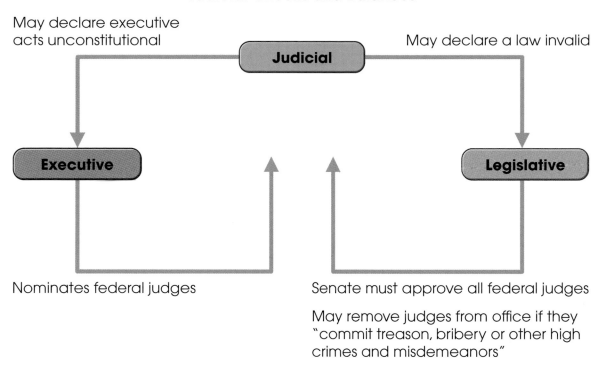

May declare executive
acts unconstitutional

Judicial

May declare a law invalid

Executive

Legislative

Nominates federal judges

Senate must approve all federal judges

May remove judges from office if they
"commit treason, bribery or other high
crimes and misdemeanors"

they have won the approval of the Senate. The legislative
branch also has the constitutional power to remove federal
judges who commit "treason, bribery, or other high crimes
and misdemeanors."

Judicial and Executive Checks

Just as the Supreme Court can declare laws passed by the
legislative branch unconstitutional, it can declare acts of the
executive branch unconstitutional.

The executive branch has a check on the judicial branch
through the president's power to nominate federal judges. This
is an important power because presidents can choose
candidates who hold political beliefs similar to their own. In this
way, they can influence the way federal courts, including the
Supreme Court, will decide future cases.

In the next section, you will learn how the first **Congress**
organized the judicial branch.

The Organization of the Judicial Branch

As you have read, the Constitution states that the judicial branch of the United States government should consist of a supreme court and other lower courts created by Congress. In 1789, Congress passed the Judiciary Act, which divided the nation into thirteen judicial districts, or areas. Each district had its own federal judge.

Congress then divided the thirteen districts into three regions, called **circuits**. The regions were called circuits because the Judiciary Act required Supreme Court justices to periodically travel along a circuit, or route, to hear cases along with the **district court** judges. Members of Congress thought that allowing the public to see the nation's highest judges and the workings of the court would inspire respect for the court and give authority to the judicial branch.

The Judicial Branch After 1789

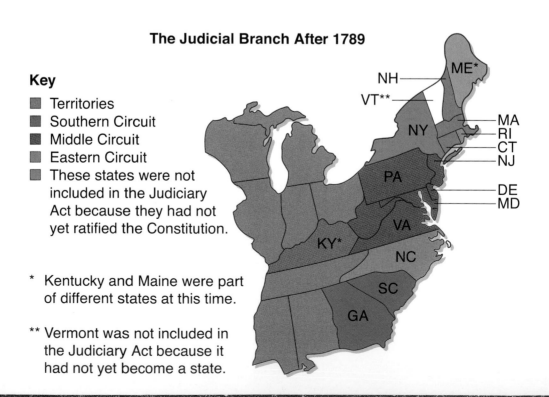

Key

- ■ Territories
- ■ Southern Circuit
- ■ Middle Circuit
- ■ Eastern Circuit
- ■ These states were not included in the Judiciary Act because they had not yet ratified the Constitution.

* Kentucky and Maine were part of different states at this time.

** Vermont was not included in the Judiciary Act because it had not yet become a state.

However, the justices quickly grew to dislike circuit riding. In the early years of the Supreme Court, there were no railroads, cars, or planes. Roads were often in poor condition, and justices traveled in carriages or on horseback. Some justices had accidents and suffered physical injuries. A runaway horse-and-carriage crushed the leg of Justice James Iredell. Another justice, Salmon Chase, nearly died after falling into Pennsylvania's Susquehanna River.

◀ Circuit riding was disliked by Supreme Court justices because traveling was very difficult during the time. One justice complained that riding many hours in a horse-and-carriage gave him "a rattling distracting noise in [his] head."

To reduce the workload of the justices, Congress added another justice to the Supreme Court whenever a new federal circuit was created. By 1862, the Supreme Court had ten justices, one more than it has today.

The judicial branch continued to grow, and the number of cases it handled increased. The courts gradually became overwhelmed. In 1891, Congress passed the Circuit Court of Appeals Act, which reduced the number of cases that the federal judiciary examined. It also ended circuit riding.

Federal Courts vs. State Courts

The current structure of the federal judicial system grew out of Congress's original division of judicial districts. Today, we have a Supreme Court, 13 **Courts of Appeals**, 94 district courts (also called **trial** courts), and 2 courts that hear special cases. Congress has the power to create or **abolish** any federal court except the Supreme Court.

There are also courts outside the federal judicial system, called state courts. Their structure is very similar to the structure of the federal judicial branch, but in some states the different levels of courts have different names. For example, trial courts may be called courts of common plea, and courts of appeal may be called superior courts or commonwealth courts.

The main difference between the federal and state courts is the types of cases they hear. The federal

The Federal Judiciary Today

Key
- D.C. Circuit
- First Circuit
- Second Circuit
- Third Circuit
- Fourth Circuit
- Fifth Circuit
- Sixth Circuit
- Seventh Circuit
- Eighth Circuit
- Ninth Circuit
- Tenth Circuit
- Eleventh Circuit

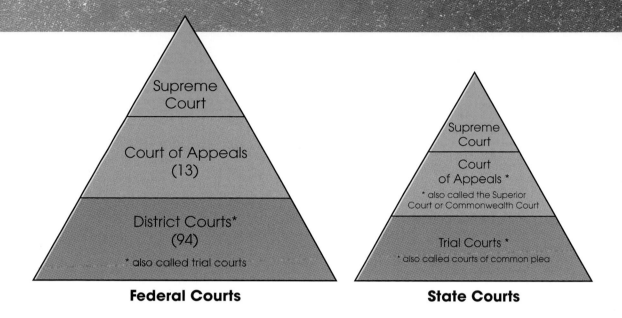

Federal Courts

State Courts

courts have **jurisdiction** over cases involving federal law. In other words, they have the power to rule over cases that involve laws or rights set forth by the national government and the U.S. Constitution. Federal courts also hear cases involving people from two different states, or someone suing a person from a foreign country. In both of these types of cases, the person must be suing for at least $75,000 for the case to be heard in a federal court. Other federal cases include disputes over money between the U.S. government and other countries and cases involving the U.S. military.

All other cases may be heard in the state courts. State courts have jurisdiction over cases involving a state law. They handle small legal disputes between individuals, or minor violations, such as parking tickets. However, they also hear cases involving more serious violations, such as criminal trials.

Together, federal and state courts ensure that citizens have a place to take all kinds of legal matters. In the next section, you will learn more about the lowest level of courts in the federal judicial branch.

The District Courts

The lowest courts in the judicial branch are the district courts, where trials are held. As you have read, there are 94 district courts in the United States and its territories, with at least one district in each state. The boundaries of a district are determined by population and the number of cases judges hear. Smaller states usually have only one judicial district, while larger states, like California and Texas, have several districts.

Generally, trials for two kinds of cases are held in district courts: criminal cases and civil cases.

Criminal Cases

In criminal cases, the government—through a United States **attorney**—seeks to **convict** those suspected of committing a crime. Criminal trials are presented before a judge and **jury**. A jury is a group of citizens selected to hear a trial. They listen to the **evidence** presented by the attorneys from each side and then decide whether the **defendant** is innocent or guilty.

The U.S. attorney's role is to prove beyond a reasonable doubt that the defendant is guilty. To do this, the attorney must present evidence that is so strong no reasonable person would doubt that the defendant committed the crime. If the jury reaches a **verdict** (decision) of "not guilty," the defendant is free to go. If the jury finds the defendant guilty of the crime, then the judge determines a punishment. Depending on the crime and the laws of the state where it was committed, punishment can range from paying a fine to being put to death.

▼ In a criminal trial, an attorney representing the U.S. government presents evidence to a jury to prove a suspect is guilty of a crime. In all U.S. courts, suspects are assumed to be "innocent until proven guilty."

Civil Cases

Civil cases involve a disagreement between two or more people or groups. They only go to trial after the **plaintiff** and defendant have tried to reach an agreement out of court and failed. In a civil case, the plaintiff accuses the defendant of doing something that is harmful or undesirable. The plaintiff must show evidence of the harm he or she has experienced, and usually asks the court for money to make up for his or her suffering. The plaintiff might also ask the court to order the defendant to stop the harmful behavior. Some civil cases are presented before a jury, while others are tried before a judge or other official.

As you have read, criminal cases require the U.S. government to prove "beyond a reasonable doubt" that the defendant is guilty of the crime. In civil cases, the **burden of proof** is lower. The plaintiff's claim must be supported by "a preponderance of the evidence." In other words, the plaintiff must prove that his or her claim is more than likely to be correct.

District courts are where a case begins, but they aren't always where a case ends. In the next section, you will learn about the courts of appeals.

▲ In 1994, ex-football star O.J. Simpson was taken to court for the murder of his former wife, Nicole Brown Simpson. When the criminal court found him not guilty of the crime, Nicole's family took Simpson to civil court, where the burden of proof is lower. The civil court found in favor of Nicole's family. It ordered Simpson to pay money to the family for their emotional distress over the crime.

The Appellate Courts

If a person disagrees with the verdict reached by a district court, he or she may then take the case to a higher court within the federal court system, called a Court of Appeals. This court will then review the case and decide whether or not to change the original verdict. In a civil case, either the plaintiff or the defendant can **appeal** the verdict. In a criminal case, only the defendant has the right to appeal.

The 94 judicial districts are divided into 12 circuits, each of which has a Court of Appeals. A Court of Appeals is also called an appellate court. There is one appellate court in the federal system that has jurisdiction in all 50 states. In other words, the circuit it serves is the whole United States. This court is called the United States Court of Appeals for the Federal Circuit and was created by Congress in 1982. It is the

▼ This is a photograph of the United States Court of Appeals for the Federal Circuit building, located in Washington, D.C.

▲ In this photograph, judges of the 9th U.S. Circuit Court of Appeals listen as an attorney argues his case.

only federal appeals court that can hear cases from all over the country. Most of the cases heard in this court are about inventions and ideas that one group is accusing another of stealing.

The Appeals Process

Appeals are heard by a panel of judges. The person or people appealing a verdict try to convince the panel that a legal error was made in the case. The person who defends the district court's decision tries to convince the panel that the original decision should stand. While considering a case, the panel of judges reviews original court materials, but it does not see new evidence or hear from witnesses.

Usually, the decision made in an appellate court is final. Sometimes, however, the panel of judges will send a case back to the district court for more investigation. The loser in an appeals case can also ask the Supreme Court to review the case.

The Supreme Court

The Supreme Court is the last resort for people who want to appeal a verdict. Every year, it receives thousands of **petitions**, or requests to hear the cases of people who were not satisfied with the decision of a lower court. Currently, the Supreme Court must review as many as 8,000 petitions each term. (The Supreme Court's term lasts from the beginning of October until the end of June or early July.) However, it does not have to hear all of these cases. It usually chooses cases that involve an important legal idea. Other times, it may decide to hear cases in which two or more appellate courts understood a law differently.

Supreme Court justices review more than 100 petitions each week. They gather in a closed conference room to discuss which cases they think the court should consider. In these meetings, the chief justice presents each case. The other justices then comment on the case in order of who has been a justice the longest. To be considered, a petition must receive at least four of the nine justices' votes. Although the

▲ Thurgood Marshall was the first African-American Supreme Court justice. He served from 1967 to 1991.

▲ Supreme Court justices meet in the conference room to choose which cases they will hear in court. These meetings are held in complete secrecy to allow the justices to express their opinions freely.

justices hold these meetings in private, the results of their votes are made public.

Once the court grants a petition, the case is put on the Supreme Court's schedule. If a petition is not granted, the decision of the lower court is final. In recent years, the justices have selected approximately 100 cases per term.

In the following section, you will learn how Supreme Court justices make decisions on the cases they choose to hear.

How the Supreme Court Decides a Case

Once the Supreme Court accepts a case, lawyers from each side have to submit documents called **briefs**. Briefs are short outlines of each lawyer's arguments. The lawyers must then appear in front of the justices to present their case. This is called an **oral argument**. The court gives each side about 30 minutes for its oral argument. During this time, the justices can interrupt and ask questions about the case.

After studying case briefs and listening to oral arguments, the justices meet together in a private session to discuss the case. Then they vote on their decision. Five justices must vote in favor of the same side in order to reach a decision. There are nine justices including the chief justice, so five out of nine votes equals a majority.

After making a decision on a case, the Supreme Court then writes an **opinion**. An opinion is a written

▼ Supreme Court justices generally hear oral arguments in public sessions held on Mondays, Tuesdays, and Wednesdays. Although the sessions are public, no photography is allowed in the courtroom.

document that explains the legal reasons and principles behind the Supreme Court's decision. If the chief justice is among the majority voters, he or she decides who will write the court's opinion. If the chief justice is in the minority, then the justice who has served the longest decides who will write the majority opinion.

It is common for justices to have differing views about a case. For this reason, the court often issues two other types of opinions. Justices in the minority frequently write **dissenting opinions**, which explain why they disagree with the decision. **Concurring opinions** are written by justices who agree with the majority decision, but not with the reasons behind making the decision.

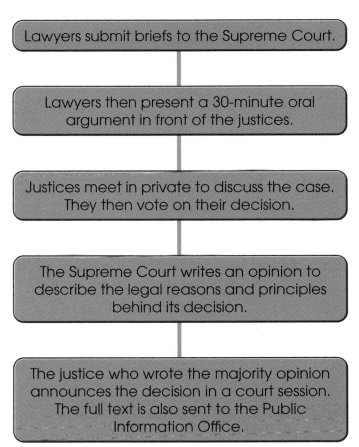

The Supreme Court Process

Lawyers submit briefs to the Supreme Court.

Lawyers then present a 30-minute oral argument in front of the justices.

Justices meet in private to discuss the case. They then vote on their decision.

The Supreme Court writes an opinion to describe the legal reasons and principles behind its decision.

The justice who wrote the majority opinion announces the decision in a court session. The full text is also sent to the Public Information Office.

The justice assigned to writing the opinion often asks for comments from other justices before a final opinion is published. When a final decision has been reached, the justice who wrote the opinion announces the decision in a court session. The court also issues the full text of the opinion to the public through its Public Information Office.

Once the Supreme Court issues an opinion, the decision is final. It can be changed only through an amendment to the Constitution or a new decision by the Supreme Court. Lower courts are required to follow the Supreme Court's decision in deciding related cases in the future.

Miranda vs. Arizona (1966)

This decision established that police must inform criminal suspects of their Fifth Amendment rights. These include a suspect's right to a lawyer and the right to refuse to answer questions or give evidence that might incriminate him or her.

Arizona police arrested Ernesto Miranda because he was suspected of serious crimes. The police questioned him for two hours, and Miranda later signed a written confession. But the police had not informed Miranda of his rights before the interrogation. So the court said that prosecutors could not use Miranda's confession as evidence at his trial. The court also outlined the kinds of warnings police should give suspects in the future, such as the right to remain silent and the right to have an attorney present during interrogations.

▼ In 1966, the Supreme Court ruled in favor of Ernesto Miranda (right), who was questioned by police officers before they read him his rights. This court decision dramatically changed what evidence could be used in court.

Bush vs. Gore (2000)

In the 2000 presidential election, Vice President Al Gore ran against challenger George W. Bush. The race was very close, and came down to which candidate had won the most votes in the state of Florida. Florida election officials said that Bush had won by fewer than 2,000 votes.

Because the vote was so close, Florida officials were required to recount the votes. The recount showed that Bush had won by fewer than 400 votes. However, the counting machines had rejected tens of thousands of votes. Some ballots were not

▲ Gore and Bush supporters wait outside the Supreme Court building during the hearing on the Florida vote recount.

marked clearly enough for the machines to read. Gore asked for a hand recount, which would include the rejected ballots. Bush argued that this would be unfair.

The Supreme Court decided to hear the case, and ruled in Bush's favor. It ordered the counties in Florida to stop the hand recount. The Supreme Court argued that a hand recount caused citizens' votes to be treated differently, since each county could have a different way of recounting the votes. The court based this decision on the Fourteenth Amendment of the Constitution, which guarantees citizens equal rights within their state.

Since Bush had more votes in Florida before the hand recount began, he became the 43rd president of the United States.

In these landmark cases, the Supreme Court acted as the final word on how the U.S. Constitution applies to our everyday lives, and set **precedents** for future court decisions. It continues to define the powers of the U.S. government, as well as the rights of its people.

The Supreme Court Building and A Day in the Life of a Justice

For much of its existence, the Supreme Court conducted business in a few rooms of the U.S. **Capitol**. In 1929, Congress authorized funding for the construction of a Supreme Court building. The Court began its first term in the new building in October of 1935.

Architect Cass Gilbert designed the Supreme Court building to represent a house of justice. Outside the building stand several sculptures that symbolize justice or represent the history and development of the law. The inside of the building is also filled with judicial-themed artwork. At the building's center is the courtroom where the justices hear oral arguments and issue opinions. The focus of the room is the long mahogany bench, where the justices sit. Giant columns of polished Italian marble rise up

▼ This photograph shows the chambers of the U.S. Supreme Court.

behind the bench. In front of the bench are chairs and tables for lawyers and seating for visitors. Above the room are carved panels that depict legal themes.

When court is in session, most justices arrive early, around 7 a.m. Some have breakfast with their law clerks and discuss upcoming cases or other topics of interest. Just before the justices enter the courtroom at

◀ Supreme Court justices have a very important job. Their decisions affect how the Constitution is understood today.

10 a.m. to hear oral arguments, they put on their black robes and shake each other's hands. This tradition dates back to the 1800s. It shows that even if the justices don't agree with one another, they respect each other.

Most days, justices hear oral arguments for two hours, then break for lunch at noon. At 1 p.m, the justices return to hear oral arguments for another two hours. For the rest of the evening and into the night, the justices research the issues before the court.

Court decisions have a powerful impact on the social and economic life of the United States. The justices need to be as prepared as possible to conduct the business of the Supreme Court, the final interpretor of the U.S. Constitution.

Glossary

abolish put an end to something, such as a law

appeal bring a case before a higher court to review a decision made by a lower court

attorney individual, such as a lawyer, who is appointed to conduct legal business on behalf of someone else

brief written document that argues the legal reasons why one side in a case should prevail

burden of proof duty of proving that a claim you make is true

Capitol building of the legislative branch

checks and balances system that makes sure one branch of government cannot become stronger than another branch

chief justice head of the Supreme Court

circuit region that encompasses a number of judicial districts and which has a court that hears appeals from its district courts

civil rights movement period of history that began in the 1950s in which blacks sought racial equality through nonviolent protest

concurring opinion opinion written by a judge who agrees with the decision of the majority, but not with the reasons given for that decision

Congress legislative branch of the United States that has two houses: the Senate and the House of Representatives

constitution document containing a country's basic principles and laws; it describes the powers and duties of the government

convict declare a person guilty of a crime in a court of law

Court of Appeals court in the federal judicial system that has the authority to hear appeals from lower courts, including the district courts

defendant person required to answer criminal or civil charges in a court

dissenting opinion opinion written by a judge who disagrees with the decision of the majority district

district court trial court in the federal judicial system

evidence objects or information used to prove the guilt of someone accused of a crime

executive branch part of the government that carries out and enforces laws

federal of or relating to the national government as distinct from the state governments

federal system system in which power is divided between national and state governments

judicial branch part of the government that interprets the law

judicial review power of the Supreme Court to revoke laws and acts of the government

jurisdiction power a court has to rule over certain kinds of cases

jury group of citizens selected to hear a trial

justice judge of the Supreme Court

legislative branch part of the government that makes laws

opinion written or oral explanation of the legal reasons upon which a decision of the court is based

oral argument verbal presentation given in court of legal reasons that one side in a case should prevail

petition written request asking a court for a specific judicial action

plaintiff person who begins a lawsuit against another person or party in a civil court

precedent legal decision in an earlier case that judges and lawyers use to evaluate similar cases in the future

segregation isolation of a group of people brought about by forcing the group to live in certain areas or by preventing its members from using facilities used by others

separation of powers system of government that distributes power between several branches

Supreme Court highest federal court in the United States

term length of time, set by law, served by an elected person

trial hearing of a case in a court of law

unconstitutional in disagreement with the principles or laws in the Constitution

verdict decision made by a jury in a court of law

Further Reading

Giesecke, Ernestine. *National Government*. Chicago: Heinemann Library, 2004.

Lawson, Dawn. *Landmark Supreme Court Cases*. New Jersey: Enslow, 1987.

Rappaport, Doreen. *Tinker vs. Des Moines: Student Rights on Trial*. New York: Harper Collins, 1993.

Index